You're Not
Mad
Enough Yet

BY

THE PEOPLE'S VOICE TO CONGRESS, LLC

authorHOUSE®

AuthorHouse™
1663 Liberty Drive, Suite 200
Bloomington, IN 47403
www.authorhouse.com
Phone: 1-800-839-8640

First published by AuthorHouse 5/15/2008

ISBN: 978-1-4343-7712-8 (sc)
ISBN: 978-1-4343-7711-1 (hc)

Library of Congress Control Number: 2008902252

Printed in the United States of America
Bloomington, Indiana

This book is printed on acid-free paper.

THANKS TO MY WONDERFUL WIFE,
VICTORIA, FOR HER SUPPORT, DEDICATION,
UNDERSTANDING, CONTRIBUTIONS, AND
PUTTING UP WITH ME
AS I WROTE THIS BOOK,

DEDICATED TO THE CITIZENS OF THE UNITED STATES WHO DESERVE FAR BETTER REPRESENTATION FROM THE SENATE AND THE HOUSE OF REPRESENTATIVES THAN THEY ARE PRESENTLY GETTING.

WHAT DOES IT TAKE

TO GET YOU

MAD ENOUGH

TO TAKE ACTION

AND DEMAND THE CHANGES

THAT NEED TO BE MADE

BY OUR ELECTED

REPRESENTATIVES

TO PROTECT YOUR INTEREST?

Table of Contents

FOREWORD

I am just an ordinary guy, seventy-four years old. I spent forty-three years pursuing my career. I am now a retired professional and business executive.

I lived through the Second World War, the Korean Conflict, the Vietnam War, the other police actions and conflicts of the time, the Gulf Wars, and am now living through the wars in Afghanistan and Iraq.

I have lived through the social, economic, and political changes from the forties through today. I am not happy with the course of change I see happening in our country today.

There is nothing else you need to know about me. What you need to do is think about the matters that need changing in our country today, and then take action to make those changes happen.

Our elected senators and representatives are supposed to be protecting our country and our citizens, and passing legislation in the best interest

of all our citizens. Instead, they seem to spend the majority of their time protecting themselves, playing partisan politics, and assuring their re-election. Read the proposed issue solutions I refer to in the chapters in this book, and you judge for yourself whether you believe they are protecting you or themselves.

I do not intend to be politically correct in my comments in this book, as I believe political correctness is the wrong path for us to be on.

I will express my views as to what legislation needs to be passed and what other actions need to be taken to put our country back on the right path for the future.

I am not trying to convince you that my suggestions are the correct ones. Rather, I write this to make you think about these subjects and come to your own conclusions. If you have better solutions, great; then become active by submitting them to the Senate and the House of Representatives, to bring about the changes that need to be made to protect our country, our way of life, and our freedoms.

The proposed issue solutions, discussed in the following chapters, have no relationship to whether you are a democrat or a republican, or are liberal or conservative.

Most of the suggested changes discussed in the following chapters are my own ideas. I have discussed them with many people over the years. Some of the suggested changes I have heard in other discussions. I have expanded on them and put them into my own words of suggested changes. I have sent some of these suggestions to various senators, representatives, and other think tanks for their consideration.

I am not aware there is anything in this book that would in any way constitute a violation of copyright laws.

I thought about writing this book many years ago, but for whatever reason, I never got around to it. I decided at this stage of my life that I would quit procrastinating, write the book, and get it published.

Whether or not it becomes successful or makes a contribution to our society is up to you.

PROLOGUE

At about the time our original thirteen states adopted their new constitution in the year 1787, Alexander Tyler (a Scottish history professor at the University of Edinborough) had this to say about the fall of the Athenian Republic some 2,000 years earlier:

> *A democracy is always temporary in nature; it simply cannot exist as a permanent form of government. A democracy will continue to exist up until the time that voters discover that they can vote themselves generous gifts from the public treasury. From that moment on, the majority always votes for candidates who promise the most benefits from the public treasury, with the result that every democracy will finally collapse due to loose fiscal policy, which is always followed by a dictatorship.*

> *The average age of the world's greatest civilizations, from the beginning of history, has been about 200 years. During those 200*

years, these nations always progressed through
the following sequence:
  From bondage to spiritual faith;
  From spiritual faith to great courage;
  From courage to liberty;
  From liberty to abundance;
  From abundance to complacency;
  From complacency to apathy;
  From apathy to dependence;
  From dependency back into bondage.

The above quotes are probably fictitious. "There was a Scottish Lord, 'Lord Woodhouselee, Alexander Fraser Tytler' who was a Scottish Historian/Proffesor who wrote several books in that time frame talking about universal history which contained extensive discussions of the political systems in historic civilizations including Athens." The sequences make logical sense. We will stay with this quote from Alexander Tytler, as taken from the internet (author unknown), even though it is probably ficticious.

Views have been expressed that the U.S. is now somewhere between the complacency and apathy phase of Professor Tylers definition of democracy; with some 40 percent of the nations population already having reached the governmental dependency phase.

If all this is true, we have reason to have great concern about the direction our country is heading in. We had better come to grips with the action we need to take to put our country back on the right path.

CHAPTER 1

THE ILLEGAL IMMIGRATION SOLUTION

1. Put a freeze on all immigration into the U.S. until we fully secure our borders.

2. Pass a law designating any foreign nationals who are currently in the U.S. illegally as felons. Have the provision of the felony status to become effective one year after passage of the law.

3. During the one-year period:

   a. Shut down the borders completely;

   b. Establish a new, detailed, and well-administered guest worker program. The new program should provide for a special, tamper-proof, numbered identification card, with a name, a picture, and fingerprints. This card is to be issued to any foreign individual, clearly identifying the individual as a foreign national under the guest worker program. If the guest worker is given a limited driver's license, such individual would have to pass an applicable driver's written examination in English and the physical driver's test. The license should specifically state that the license does not entitle the individual to vote in any election in the United States, either federal or state. Once under the guest worker program, the individual will have to provide an address and telephone number where the individual lives in the U.S., and where the individual works. The individual will be required to register any change of address or change of employment. Failure to comply with the requirements would mean permanent loss of guest worker status. All employers would be required to register the employment of such guest workers and pay all applicable taxes. All employers would be required to pay such workers, under the guest worker program, at least the applicable minimum wage and provide healthcare benefits, the same as their other employees.

c. All foreign nationals who are here illegally will be given the opportunity to register with an appointed government agency, providing name, picture, fingerprints, DNA, and background information, including criminal information. Once they register, they are to leave the United States. If they leave the United States, as required, they will be placed on a list in the order of their registration. When the new guest worker program is put into effect, if they meet the legal qualification requirements (no criminal activity or drug involvement), they will be given preference for guest worker status in the order of their registration time and date, and will be allowed to apply under applicable laws for citizenship (no status preference applicable here; they will have to start at the back of the line);

d. Any foreign nationals entering the United States illegally after the law is passed, as provided in paragraph 2 above, shall automatically become felons and forever lose all rights to guest worker status or U.S. citizenship.

4. The reason for the felon status under the law is as follows: Most foreign nationals want to come to the U.S. for jobs, and ultimately, citizenship. They can do so if they comply with the law. If they fail to comply with the law,

they will become felons and are then subject to prosecution, jail time, and after that, deportation. Once they become a felon, they give up the opportunity forever for guest worker status and citizenship. This incentive alone will guarantee that the non-criminals will follow the law. No amnesty is given to anyone under any conditions. We have done this in the past and it did not work.

5. Amend Section 1 of the Fourteenth Amendment of the Constitution to preclude automatic citizenship of children born in the United States of foreign nationals, whether they are here legally, under a guest worker program, or illegally. Clarify the phrase in the first sentence of the Fourteenth Amendment "subject to the jurisdiction thereof" to make it clear that this phrase does not apply to any foreign nationals who are in this country legally, under a guest worker program, or illegally. In the interim, while the Fourteenth Amendment is in the process of being amended, pass a law revising the interpretation of the language in the first sentence of the Fourteenth Amendment, whereby it had been ruled that such citizenship should be granted.

Rewrite the immigration laws, revising the number of immigrants allowed in the U.S. each year back to the previous number before it was increased, and make them much stricter. Strictly enforce the immigration laws.

Pass a law establishing penalties against employers that hire illegal immigrants, and banks and lending institutions that loan money to illegal immigrants to purchase homes, cars, or for other purposes. The monetary penalty should be no less than $50,000 for each violation.

Pass a law providing that foreign nationals, guest workers, and illegal immigrants shall not receive social security benefits, free medical benefits, free education, or any other welfare benefits.

This is the only effective solution to the illegal immigration problem in the U.S., and to effectively eliminate the outrageous cost to the taxpayers of their permitted existence here.

Facts you should know: The Heritage Foundation scholar, Robert Rector, estimates the price tag for the proposed immigration bill that was defeated in the Senate at 2.5 trillion dollars—with a capital T. A provision of the proposed legislation—which was only reported on by one talk-show host—

would have provided immediate coverage to all illegal immigrants under the affirmative action laws and would have given all of them minority preference status for all federal and state civil-service jobs, including police and fire positions. I am not sure our country could have survived the ultimate result of such application.

How dare the Senate and the House put that kind of financial burden on the taxpayers of the United States?

Even if a new law is passed, these recommendations should be put in place to be applicable against the next wave of illegal immigrants who will be crossing our borders in the future. They will still be coming over believing that we will continue to give them amnesty and let them stay in our country as we always have.

Looking back, the American Indian would certainly have concerns about uncontrolled immigration. Since they were not organized as one nation, they lost a lot. Since we are one nation, we do have the ability to better protect ourselves.

The Founding Fathers were not very positive about the issue of immigration; in fact, they had significant concerns with respect to any immigrants where the cultural and social background was markedly different from their own.

CHAPTER 2

INTERNATIONAL HIGHWAY

1. Our government is planning on building an international highway from Mexico, through the United States, to Canada.

2. This highway should be stopped at all cost. It is an open invitation to non-U.S. citizens and terrorists to enter the country by illegal means, and to the drug lords to ship more drugs into the country.

3. There is no way you can police all of the miles of this highway, and these entities will find a way to use it to their benefit and to our detriment.

4. We are playing right into their hands by such undertaking.

5. It gives credence to the desires of Mexico to have Mexico, the United States, and Canada become the American Union, similar to the European Union. This is not in our best interest.

CHAPTER 3

TAX CUTS

1. Make all the federal tax cuts permanent. The evidence is overwhelming that tax cuts are best for the economy and the people.

2. Pass the Fair Tax Act. Eliminate the IRS. Eliminate the inheritance tax and all other taxes, except a Sales Tax. The only tax would be a sales tax. This would eliminate tax-incentive legislation for special interest groups, and eliminate a large segment of lobbyists. That would help solve many of the ethical problems facing our elected officials.

3. Abolish the Sixteenth Amendment of the Constitution, thereby precluding Congress from passing any legislation implementing or approving any other form of taxes, direct, indirect, or under any other name or in any form whatsoever. The states will follow suit and pass state fair tax legislation, also.

At this point, I thought it might be enlightening for all of you to realize that, at some point in your life you may be paying as many as 44 different federal and state taxes.

It is also important to note that none of these taxes existed 100 years ago. Our nation was doing well and on its way to becoming the most prosperous in the world. We had absolutely no national debt, well on our way to creating the largest middle class in the world, and Mom stayed home to raise the kids.

What happened? Could it be the proliferation and impact of politicians?

And we still have to "press 1" for English.

CHAPTER 4

SPENDING CUTS

1. Tax cuts are not enough. We need spending cuts also.

2. Every government agency and every program should be reviewed, and those that are not serving **"an absolutely necessary purpose"** should be abolished. **"An absolutely necessary purpose" should be strictly interpreted.**

3. The annual budget of all remaining agencies should be reduced by 20 percent the first year, except for the military budget. Every year thereafter, the annual budgets of each agency should be reviewed strictly and reduced as much as possible.

4. The military budget should be increased appropriately, until such time as the size (see chapter 22), capability, and weaponry are at the appropriate level to provide full protection of our country. Thereafter, the military budget

should be maintained at an appropriate level to assure the size, capability, and weaponry are maintained at such level.

5. No "earmarks" or "pork-barrel" spending should be allowed to be tacked on to other proposed legislation. So far in 2007, the House of Representatives included $4.2 billion in earmarks. You, the taxpayer, are paying for this. The members of the Appropriations Committee, the ones who hand out the earmarks, are the worst violators.

6. No new programs, especially welfare programs, can be established unless they meet the standards of **"an absolutely necessary purpose."**

7. The budgets for the staffs of the senators and representatives should be cut by 20 percent in the first year. Every year thereafter, the annual budgets of each member of each senator and representative's staff should be reviewed strictly and reduced as much as possible.

CHAPTER 5

CIVIL SERVANTS

Over the next few years, a large number of civil servants will be retiring. We need a law passed in both the Senate and the House establishing the principle that none of the positions of retired civil servants will be filled. Any additions to the civil-servant staff of any agency will have to be strictly reviewed by both the Senate and the House. Before such additions can be approved, the requesting agency will have to make budget cuts in their budget to offset the cost of adding additional personnel to its staff.

CHAPTER 6

WELFARE

The whole concept of "welfare" needs to be reviewed and changed. People receiving welfare should be required to work and earn their welfare benefits. There are many projects in each city that need to be taken care of, and the welfare recipients can do a lot of that work. This will cut the budgets of the cities by having the welfare recipients accomplish much of this work. Instead of paying others to do this work, the city management can use some of the money to be saved in managing the welfare recipients to accomplish this work.

CHAPTER 7

SANCTUARY STATES AND CITIES

For those states and cities that refuse to comply with the immigration laws and all other federal laws, all federal funding to such states and cities, for any purpose, will be stopped immediately, and will be denied until such states and cities establish they are in full compliance with applicable federal laws.

CHAPTER 8

FOREIGN AID

1. Our government is providing monetary aid too many countries of the world and to other specific aid programs to foreign countries. Many of these countries do not view the United States in a positive manner, and are not supportive of our country.

2. For the first year, we should cut the total foreign aid budget by 30 percent, and each year thereafter, a detailed study should be made of all foreign aid being given to each country and each program.

3. The Senate, House, and the administration should review, each year, the results of the study, and eliminate all foreign aid that is not absolutely necessary, in the best interest of our country, and to those entities that are working against the interest of the United States.

CHAPTER 9

FOREIGN TRADE

1. Our national security is far too important to place our country in a vulnerable position. No products or parts of any nature whatsoever, with respect to military planes, military equipment, or military weapons should ever be made by a non-U.S. entity, whether that entity is doing business in the U.S. or not. There should be plenty of U.S. companies competent enough to compete for this business, and if not, it is a great opportunity to create new U.S. businesses to prosper for a long time. There will always be a need for our military products and replacement parts, and it represents a great opportunity for U.S. businesses.

2. For the same national security reasons, our ports, airports, borders, all forms of transportation (planes, trains, and buses, and all other activities that may relate to national security) should be

run and managed by U.S. companies solely. No foreign entities, whether doing business in the U.S. or not, should ever be awarded a contract to run or manage any such activities.

TRADE AGREEMENTS

1. The term "trade agreements" should be revised to read "fair trade agreements" with emphasis on the word "fair."

2. Trade agreements should be fair to both parties. They should not be a one-way street or one-sided.

3. For those countries that charge tariffs when our products are to be sold in their country, we should charge corresponding tariffs on all their products to be sold in the U.S.

4. For all other "trade agreements," they should work on a fair and equal basis annually to be adjusted quarterly. For example, if country A ships 10 million dollars of goods to be sold in the U.S. in the first quarter, and the U.S. only shipped 5 million dollars of goods to be sold in country A in the first quarter, country A should be precluded from shipping any further goods to be sold in the U.S. until the U.S. has

shipped another 5 million worth of goods to be sold in country A. Once the foreign countries understand how the trade agreements work, they will have to open their markets to U.S. products if they want to continue shipping their goods to the U.S. for sale.

5. Trade agreements should not be administered in such fashion to induce U.S. products to be made in foreign countries to take advantage of cheaper labor rates. If they cannot sell the products in the U.S., they will not start producing them in their country.

6. All products to be shipped to the U.S. for sale, by plane, boat, train, or other form of transportation should be checked by an appropriate U.S. agency in the country of origin, before shipment, and checked again when it arrives in the U.S. The agency should not only determine the nature, quantity, and value of the products being shipped, but should also verify that the product meets the specifications required for the product. The lead paint problem with toys shipped from China this past year is a real example of the need for such quality verification. If the products cannot meet the specifications required, then let's keep the business in the U.S.

CHAPTER 10

SOCIAL SECURITY TRUST FUND

1. Pass a law that precludes Congress from raiding, borrowing or using, in any way, directly or indirectly, any of the funds in the Social Security Trust Fund for any purpose other than payment of social security benefits.

2. The Social Security Trust Fund should be put under the control of an independent board of trustees, answerable to the president. Congress has already established that it cannot be trusted to manage the trust fund.

3. Pass a law requiring that all funds previously borrowed or taken from the Social Security Trust Fund shall be immediately repaid in full to the fund, plus interest. The politicians have already taken and spent a whopping $2.071 trillion from the Social Security Trust Fund— and took another estimated $186 billion in the year 2007 alone.

CHAPTER 11

SOCIAL SECURITY AND MEDICARE

Passage of the Fair Tax Act would financially solve both these problems (see chapter 3).

There would be enough money from the sales taxes collected under the fair tax provisions to provide for full funding of the Social Security Trust Fund, Medicare, and free prescription drugs for the elderly. Provisions would have to be added to protect against such prescription drugs being sold or used illegally.

ADDITIONAL SOLUTION

Now, if you really want to solve the social security and Medicare problem for the future, pass the necessary laws that after term limits are voted in (see chapter 13) all newly elected senators, representatives, and other elected or appointed federal officials and their spouses will no longer receive free lucrative lifetime pensions and free lucrative lifetime medical care, paid for by the taxpayers. They would receive social security benefits and Medicare benefits like the rest of us. I guarantee you that if they are only covered by social security and Medicare, they will definitely put in place the solutions necessary to fund these programs and quit borrowing the trust fund money for other projects. They would be required to pay into the social security fund just like we do. While they are in office, they would be covered by group medical coverage, for which they would have to pay 50 percent of the cost, with the other 50 percent being paid from taxes collected. This is what I referred to in the foreword, when I said they spend their time taking care of themselves. They passed legislation providing for free pensions and free medical care for life, and we are paying for every penny of that.

ALTERNATE SOLUTION

If senators, representatives, and other elected or appointed federal officials and their spouses are not brought under the social security and Medicare programs, as an alternative, consider abolishing social security altogether.

Pensions are a thing of the past. Everyone over forty-five years of age would be grandfathered under the present social security provisions.

Everyone up to forty-five years of age would be required to provide a minimum of 20 percent of their income (remember, it is now tax-free income once the Fair Tax Act is passed) each year into a personally owned, special retirement account (similar to a 401K or IRA). Such accounts would have to be registered with the government (social security agency) by the individual and the investment entity managing the account, to assure annual compliance. The money in such accounts cannot be withdrawn until the individual reaches age sixty-five. Anyone over forty-five would also be permitted to establish and maintain such accounts to supplement their social security benefits.

CHAPTER 12

EDUCATION, STREET CRIME, DRUGS, GANGS

1. Put the draft back into effect. This is not a wartime draft, but a domestic peace corps draft.

2. All individual citizens between the ages of eighteen to twenty-three must serve three years in the service of their country in the domestic peace corps. The only exception or deferment applicable would be service in the U.S. military for a three-year period. Entrance into the program would be after high school graduation, or for those dropping out of high school, when they become eighteen years of age.

3. The purpose of the program would be to have the members of the corps assigned in teams to various cities in the U.S. (starting with the large cities and moving outward from there). Their assignment would be to clean up the streets from gangs, drugs, street crime, and debris.

They would not be assigned to the city they came from. They would be selected for the teams at random to eliminate groups known to each other being assigned to the same location.

4. The teams would be administered by officers of the state national guard. Abandoned schools, military sites, and other facilities in each city would be utilized to house these teams.

5. Pass a law to the effect that it would constitute a federal felony to harm, in any way, any member of the domestic peace corps. Have this law enforced by special federal prosecutors and special federal courts. The penalty, depending on the severity of the harm, would be a minimum of ten years with no parole or time off for good behavior, up to a maximum of the death penalty.

6. The members of the domestic peace corps would be backed up by the state national guard and local police and sheriff's departments.

7. The members of the domestic peace corps would be paid a salary, similar to that of our military personnel. This would give them a job, which they sorely need. This would get all of them involved in a positive endeavor for themselves and their country.

8. Over time, the program would instill pride in the individuals, pride in their country, and pride in the freedom we enjoy.

9. We would be giving our cities back to our law-abiding citizens and cleaning up the streets from gangs, drugs, street crime, and debris.

10. The program would be a continuous program.

11. What do we give our children in return? We give them the best education we can give them, including high school completion for those who have not completed high school. Thereafter, all those in the program who belong in college and qualify for advanced degrees would be given that opportunity. They would have to maintain at least a C average at all times.

12. For all the others, trade schools would be established to give them training and job skills so they may become productive members of society and have the opportunity to have a good job and a productive life.

13. This would be the best money the taxpayers could ever spend. Mutual respect for the law and a respectful relationship between our adult citizens and our children would be a welcome by-product.

14. The program would also solve the education problems we face for underprivileged children. All children would have the opportunity to get an education.

15. The education of our children is our only salvation.

16. Far better we pay for educating all of our own children before we pay for educating foreign nationals illegally in our country.

CHAPTER 13

TERM LIMITS

1. Term limits already exist, and for good reason. There is no need to get into a philosophical discussion about the merits of term limits. We are in a constant state of change, and the government needs to change to meet the new challenges and protect our country, our freedom, and our way of life.

2. The president can only serve two four-year terms, whether consecutive or not.

3. The administration serves at the pleasure of the president, with the advice and consent of the Senate. When a new president takes office, he or she appoints a new administration.

4. The U.S. Attorneys serve at the pleasure of the president. When a new president takes office, history establishes that some or most U.S. Attorneys are replaced by the incoming president.

5. It is virtually impossible to defeat an incumbent, especially one who has been in office for years. The campaign cost alone for a new challenger makes it even more difficult. With term limits, this problem is solved and every four years (see below), we would have one third of the Senate and House filled with new representatives, which would be a very positive step.

6. We need to place term limits on the senators. Senators can only serve two six-year terms, whether consecutive or not.

7. Amend the law to provide for congressman to serve four-year terms (instead of two-year terms). They presently spend far too much time running for re-election, rather than doing the job they were elected to do. A two-year term is far too short for them to do their job.

8. We need to place term limits on the congressmen. Congressmen can only serve three four-year terms, whether consecutive or not.

9. Have elections of senators and congressmen every four years. In this way, one-third of the Senate and the House would be replaced each election year, and two-thirds would remain until

the next election. This would provide continuity in both houses.

10. For the first few elections, the most senior of the senators and congressmen would drop out, until all senators and representatives who have exceeded the term limit have been replaced.

CHAPTER 14

CONGRESSIONAL PAY—MILITARY PAY

1. Pass a law in both houses that neither the senators nor the congressmen can pass pay increases or benefit increases for themselves, unless and until they have passed a balanced budget for the year and have also passed a line-item veto for the president so all "earmarks" or "pork-barrel" spending provisions added to proposed legislation can be stricken from the legislation by the president. The balanced budget and line-item veto laws need to be written in such fashion that they can only be revoked by a 100% vote of either the full Senate or full House, or both, as necessary..

2. Pass a law in both houses that neither the senators nor the congressmen can pass pay increases or benefit increases for themselves, unless and until they have approved appropriate pay structures, increases, and special bonuses for all our military

personnel in the active service, especially the enlisted and non-commissioned personnel, including, without limitation, retirement provisions and medical coverage for military personnel and their families, comparable in scale to the similar pay and retirement benefits the senators and congressmen presently enjoy, or will enjoy in the future. Those military personnel serving on the front line in a war theatre would also receive additional special pay and bonuses, for the length of their tour of duty in the war zone. This provision is to be written in such fashion that it can only be revoked by a 100% vote of either the full Senate or the full House, or both, as necessary.

CHAPTER 15

BALANCED BUDGET

Pass a law requiring both houses to pass a balanced budget each year. The balanced budget law shall be written in such fashion that it can only be revoked by a 100 percent vote of either the full Senate or the full House, or both, as necessary (see chapter 14).

CHAPTER 16

LINE-ITEM VETO

Pass a law in both houses for a line-item veto by the president. This will allow the president to strike specific provisions, and especially, all "earmarks" or "pork-barrel" spending provisions added to proposed legislation. The line-item veto law shall be written in such fashion that it can only be revoked by a 100 percent vote of the full Senate or the full House, or both, as may be required. This will also help to eliminate the impact of lobbyists and help solve the ethical problems facing many of our elected officials (see chapter 14).

CHAPTER 17

MULTIPLE PENSIONS

Pass a law precluding any elected or appointed federal official, or marriage partner of such official, from receiving more than one federal government pension, of any nature whatsoever, regardless of how many different elected or appointed positions they may have held, allowing for entitlement to a federal pension. Any such individual would only be entitled to receive one pension from the various plans they may be entitled under, with that one pension from the pension plan providing the highest amount.

CHAPTER 18

CONFLICT OF INTEREST

1. All members of Congress, both the Senate and the House, shall be required at all times to publicly disclose, in advance, any potential conflict of interest, directly or indirectly, of any nature whatsoever, which may arise by such individual serving on any committee of the Senate or the House, or being considered for membership of such committee. After such disclosure, such individual shall be precluded from becoming a member of such committee, or be required to resign from such committee.

2. If such individual is already a member of a committee and the conflict would be applicable to all matters to come before the committee, such individual shall immediately resign from such committee. If the potential conflict would only apply to certain limited matters that may come before the committee, such member shall

publicly disclose such potential conflict and then abstain from voting on any matter where such potential conflict would apply.

3. The definition of "conflict of interest" shall be broadly interpreted.

4. Violation of the required public disclosure of potential conflict of interest, by a senator or congressman, shall require a congressional investigation by the Senate (in the case of a senator) or the House (in the case of a representative).

5. Any such investigation shall consider the possibility of such individual being required to resign from the Senate orf the House if the first violation is found to be egregious enough. If it is a second violation such individual shall be required to resign from the Senate or the House.

6. The provision of the conflict of interest disclosure shall also apply to all senators and representatives in carrying out their obligations of the position of senator or representative they have been elected to fulfill. The provisions of paragraph 4 above shall also be applicable in all such instances.

7. All members of the Senate and House of Representatives shall be precluded from hiring any members of their families, including in-laws, nieces, nephews, cousins, or other relatives as members of their staff, as consultants, or as members of their staff or as consultants on their re-election committee. Any such activity shall constitute a conflict of interest and a violation of their ethical obligations.

8. The Senate and the House of Representatives shall pass a law banning the hiring of any family member of elected senators and representatives by any registered lobbyist or lobbying organization. The penalty for violation of this ban shall be a fine of 1 million dollars for each violation and the suspension for a period of three years of such individual or organization from functioning as a registered lobbyist.

CHAPTER 19

OATH OF OFFICE

All senators and representatives and administrative personnel shall be required to publicly take an oath of office swearing allegiance to the United States, the Constitution of the United States, the government of the United States, and the flag of the United States, above all other allegiances. Such oath shall be sworn to on the Christian Bible, not some other book of another religion. Refusal to take such oath as specifically required shall preclude such individual from holding office as a senator, representative, or member of the administration, regardless of the fact that they were elected or appointed to that position.

CHAPTER 20

UNITED NATIONS

1. It's time to rethink our relationship with the United Nations.

2. We provide the United Nations an office in New York, special accommodations to the representatives, diplomatic immunity to the representatives, overlooking parking tickets and other violations of the representatives, and on top of all that, we pay the major share of the expenses.

3. It is my opinion that the majority of our citizens believe that, in general, the United Nations membership is anti-American and the United Nations itself is a "do-nothing" organization. There are far too many scandals, ethics violations, too much corruption, and significant mismanagement of their programs.

4. The United Nations certainly has not been very supportive of the United States in recent years.

5. In my humble opinion, we have not had a strong secretary general of the United Nations since Dag Hammarskjold, who served from 1953 to 1961. He died in a plane crash in September of 1961. Thirty-six years without a strong secretary general is not a good thing for the United Nations or the United States. There is far too much politics by too many countries not supportive of the United States. If we cut off paying the majority share of the cost, have the offices relocated outside of the United States, and cut back or eliminate foreign aid to all or many of these countries, maybe they will get the message and start respecting and supporting the United States. We do not require that of them now and we should.

6. It's time for the United Nations to relocate their offices to another country (say some country in Africa). It's also time for the United States to just pay its fair share of the expenses and all the other countries to start paying their fair share.

CHAPTER 21

WAR ON TERROR

1. Let's quit kidding ourselves. Radical Muslims—the terrorists—are at war with us and anyone else who does not agree with them and their religious beliefs.

2. The radical Islamic war has been going on for thousands of years. Afghanistan and Iraq are just specific fronts of the overall war. We must stay in Afghanistan and Iraq and win the war against the terrorists. If we do not win, we send them a message that we are weak, and strengthen their resolve to win. They are already here in our country and will continue with their war against us unless we win on all fronts.

3. Yes, the war in Iraq has gone on longer than World War II. We have forgotten that President Roosevelt was very unpopular during that war, as is any president during any war.

4. World War II lasted about four years. We had many more allies participating with us in that war. There were more than 25.1 million military deaths on both sides. Germany had more than 5.5 million, China had more than 3.8 million, Russia had more than 10.7 million, the United Kingdom had more than 382,000, and the United States had more than 407,000

5. In the invasion of Normandy, we lost more than five thousand of our brave soldiers that day alone, and thank God, we saved the world from the insane ambitions of Germany and Japan.

We are facing the same insanity by the radical Islamic terrorists. Even with the length of both wars in Afghanistan and Iraq, our total losses to date do not exceed the losses we suffered in the first six months of the European invasion.

6. This is not meant to justify the losses of our brave and courageous military personnel. Our military personnel are doing an outstanding job, and deserve the utmost respect of all the citizens of our country. They have volunteered to protect our country and our way of life. The comparative facts are just meant to put matters into perspective from the standpoint of a long and difficult war. The war on terror is a far

different kind of war than that of the Second World War.

7. We are not students of history. What is the old saying? It is something to the effect of, "Those who refuse to study history are doomed to repeat it." There is literature in the marketplace that provides, in great detail, analysis of the mistakes that were made, after the First World War, by the British Empire, France, the United States, and all our other allies. These mistakes ultimately allowed Adolf Hitler and Benito Mussolini to come to power. If we compare those mistakes to what is transpiring today, it would be very easy to conclude that we are well on the path of making those same, or similar, mistakes again with respect to the matters dealing with the Middle East and the terrorists.

8. What will it take to wake us up? Will it take another major attack against us on our homeland? Will it take wiping out one or more of our major cities, shopping centers, or thousands of our citizens with an atomic bomb?

9. Wake up, people! We are at war, and it is a war we must win.

CHAPTER 22

THE LAWS OF THE UNITED STATES

1. The laws of the United States are the only laws applicable to all citizens in the United States.

2. Recently, there have been articles in the news that certain Muslim leaders, clerics, and individuals are demanding that Islamic Sharia Law be applicable to them while living in the United States.

3. In my opinion, we along with a lot of other countries, have great concerns about radical Muslims coming into our country and planning to carry our terrorist attacks.

4. It is disappointing that the Muslim leaders and clerics have not taken a strong stand publicly against radical Muslim beliefs and activities worldwide, and particularly, in the United States.

5. We should have a law requiring all Muslims becoming citizens of the United States to swear allegiance to the United States, the Constitution of the United States, the government of the United States, the flag of the United States, and the laws of the United States. They will so swear allegiance on the Christian Bible and not the Koran. The law needs to make it clear that under **NO** circumstances will Sharia Law be applicable to anyone in the United States under any circumstances. They must abide by that oath at all times. If they are not willing to take such an oath, they will not be granted citizenship. This is not discriminatory; such an oath is applicable to all individuals who wish to become citizens.

CHAPTER 23

SIZE OF OUR MILITARY FORCES

1. We should add another four or five divisions to the size of our military forces.

2. The Senate and the House should approve a military budget each year to maintain such a force with the latest state-of-the-art weapons, equipment, and supplies.

3. Our only ability to preserve our freedom, our way of life, and our country is to have a military force that is capable of defeating anyone or everyone out there, especially our avowed enemies.

CHAPTER 24

TREATMENT OF CAPTURED COMBATANTS

AND TERRORISTS

1. For those captured combatants in uniform from a country that is a signatory of the Geneva Convention, they will not be afforded rights under the U.S. Constitution, but will be afforded all the rights under the Geneva Convention. They are not citizens of the United States and have no rights under our constitution.

2. For those captured combatants in uniform from a country that is not a signatory of the Geneva Convention, they will not be afforded rights under the U.S. Constitution or the Geneva Convention. They will be treated under our special laws for the handling of such captured combatants and terrorists. They are not citizens of the United States and have no rights under our constitution.

3. For captured combatants not in uniform, and all captured terrorists, they will not be afforded rights under the U.S. Constitution or the Geneva Convention. They will be treated under our special laws for the handling of such combatants and terrorists. They are not citizens of the United States and have no rights under our constitution.

4. For those U.S. citizens who join terrorist organizations, thereby becoming terrorists, they forgo their U.S. citizenship and will be treated as captured combatants not in uniform.

CHAPTER 25

ENGLISH LANGUAGE

1. Pass a law making English the official language of the United States. All United States citizens must learn to speak English fluently.

2. Include in the law provisions barring the federal government and all state and local governments from printing and distributing ballots for any elections for federal, state or local offices in any language other than English.

3. Include in the law provisions barring the federal government and all state and local governments from providing interpreters or translators, using taxpayer funds to assist people who are not able to speak English.

CHAPTER 26

AFFIRMATIVE ACTION LAWS

Abolish all federal and state Affirmative Action laws; they are long since outdated. There are enough laws on the books to protect against discrimination in the workplace.

One unintended consequences would be the application of the Affirmative Action laws to all illegal immigrants if they were to be given amnesty. (See chapter 1)

CHAPTER 27

ENERGY SOLUTION

1. The president of the United States and his selected staff should arrange a meeting with the president of Mexico and his selected staff, and the prime minister of Canada and his selected staff, to discuss and negotiate a contract whereby the United States would purchase all its oil needs from the two countries.

2. Both Mexico and Canada have enormous oil reserves, enough to cover their own needs for the future and those of the United States. The United States should purchase all its oil needs from Mexico and Canada at a fixed purchase price, together with the United States furnishing technology, to the extent necessary, to allow both countries to improve their exploration, oil production, and refinement capability.

3. This would allow the United States to eliminate its dependency on Middle Eastern oil and stem

the flow of billions of dollars into the Middle Eastern coffers. It is best that we put that money in North America and assist the economies of Mexico and Canada. This action would help to break the Middle Eastern oil cartel.

4. At the same time, the United States should plan on building at least one or more nuclear reactors every three years, thus, over time, eliminating our dependence on oil for our energy needs. Nuclear reactor technology is much improved and far safer today and the risk is low for converting to nuclear power capability.

CHAPTER 28

CONGRESSIONAL WORKING REQUIREMENTS

There is literature in the marketplace citing facts and figures establishing that the members of the Senate and the House of Representatives actually worked in session less than 50 percent of the time.

Let's set new working requirements for all members of the Senate and the House of Representatives.

They get the months of August and December off. That is nine weeks' vacation. Far better than most of us get, but let's stay with that.

That leaves forty-three weeks in which they will have to work. Now let's require all of them to be on the floor in the Senate and the House, to conduct business, four days of each of the forty-three weeks. That would leave them with a three-day weekend each week to visit home and their constituents. Now, that is not asking much, and we are entitled to ask and expect them to work in representing all of us. Under this formula, they would be working about 58 percent of the time, hopefully looking out for your interests and the interests of our country.

If any of them fails to meet the working requirement in the first year, they will forfeit any committee chair position they hold. If they fail to meet the working requirement a second time, they would be required to resign..

CHAPTER 29

PRESIDENT

Let's really get you to thinking now.

All the partisan politics over the past twenty-four years, or more, has unfortunately changed the political scene in a very negative way. Let's get it back on course.

How about a one-term president?

Change the law and have the president serve a term of six years. The president can only serve one term in his or her lifetime. The president would have six years to make his or her mark in history.

Upon being elected president, he or she must resign from any political party affiliations. He or she cannot campaign for anyone. The president would represent all the people and be in a position to stay out of partisan politics.

The vice president and the people appointed to the administration must also resign from any party affiliations. The vice president and any member of the administration who wishes to run for the presidency would resign on or before the fifth year of the presidency, or at least a year before they formally announce running or another political office, so they can run their political campaign. The president would have the sole authority to replace the vice president, with a person of his or her choice. With the advice and consent of the Senate, the president would have the authority to replace the other administrative personnel who may have resigned to run for political office.

CHAPTER 30

WHAT'S NEXT?

What happens next is all up to **you.**

It is your country, your government, and your vote. This year, we firmly established that your combined voices can command the elected senators and representatives to take the action you demand. You defeated the proposed immigration amnesty legislation that was on its way to passage. Congratulations—great job.

You can't stop here. You need to continue demanding action by the elected representatives to take the action you believe is necessary and in the best interests of all the people.

Let your senators and representatives know what it is that you want them to do. If you have better ideas than the ones presented in this book, let them know what those ideas are. If you agree with the ideas presented in this book, let them know that also.

Better yet, buy extra copies of this book and send one to each of your senators and your representatives. If everyone did this, you would have a real chance of having these proposed laws and action put in place.

I, for one, will send a copy of this book to my two senators, my representative, and also to the majority and minority leaders of both the Senate and the House of Representatives.

The future of our country, our way of life, and the English language is in your hands and up to you.

As the author of this book, I chose the name *The People's Voice to Congress* on purpose, to convey the point that when you communicate with your elected representatives, it is truly the people's voice to Congress.

God bless all of you.